The Life of Jesus
Through the eyes of an artist

Based on original paintings by Paul Forsey

About the artist

Paul is a full time artist and designer. He trained in Fine Art, painting and printmaking, at the University of Reading and is also a qualified teacher of Art and Design. He has exhibited regularly and has work in many collections including the Arthur Andersen Art Collection, P and O, the Gyosei International College and a series of ten works on paper in the Strand Headquarters of Enterprise Oil. His religious paintings have been exhibited in church buildings all over the England including Douai Abbey, Sheffield Catholic Cathedral, Lincoln Cathedral, Wells Cathedral and York Minster. If you would like to find out more about Paul's work please visit www.stepintothepicture.co.uk

Introduction

'The Life of Jesus' provides a unique opportunity for children to experience the story of Jesus' life through the vibrant and evocative contemporary art of a single artist. Aimed at 7-11s and those who teach them, the material is based on original artwork by the artist, Paul Forsey.

Each key event in Jesus' life has been interpreted through Paul's vibrant four-colour artwork and explored in further depth through the accompanying teaching material and background notes which guide the teacher and the child through the resource.

With 22 full-page four-colour plates, this book aims to encourage children to explore the different aspects of the life of Jesus in an open and critical way, as well as exploring what the artist may be trying to say through his work.

Contents

The birth of Jesus is announced

LUKE 1:26–31

One month later God sent the angel Gabriel to the town of Nazareth in Galilee with a message for a virgin named Mary. She was engaged to Joseph from the family of King David. The angel greeted Mary and said, 'You are truly blessed! The Lord is with you.'

Mary was confused by the
angel's words and wondered what they meant.
Then the angel told Mary, 'Don't be afraid! God is pleased
with you, and you will have a son. His name will be Jesus.'

Joseph dreams

MATTHEW 1:18–21

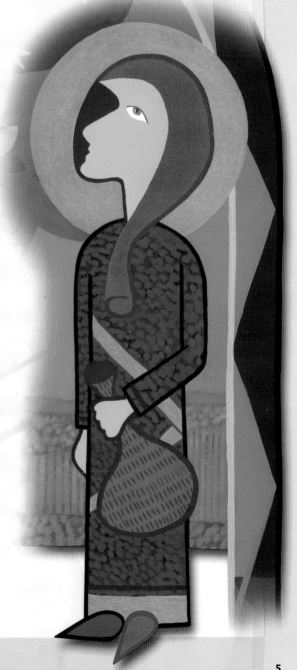

Mary was engaged to Joseph from King David's family. But before they were married, she learnt that she was going to have a baby by God's Holy Spirit. Joseph was a good man and did not want to embarrass Mary in front of everyone. So he decided to call off the wedding quietly.

While Joseph was thinking about this, an angel from the Lord came to him in a dream. The angel said, 'Joseph, the baby that Mary will have is from the Holy Spirit. Go ahead and marry her. Then after her baby is born, name him Jesus, because he will save his people from their sins.'

The birth of Jesus

LUKE 2:1–19

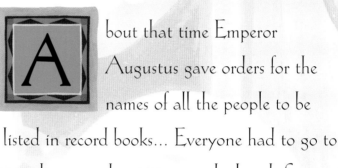

About that time Emperor Augustus gave orders for the names of all the people to be listed in record books... Everyone had to go to their own home town to be listed. So Joseph had to leave Nazareth in Galilee and go to Bethlehem in Judea... Mary was engaged to Joseph and travelled with him to Bethlehem... While they were there, she gave birth to her firstborn son. She dressed him in baby clothes and laid him on a bed of hay, because there was no room for them in the inn.

That night in the fields near Bethlehem some shepherds were guarding their sheep. All at once an angel came down to them from the Lord, and the brightness of the Lord's glory flashed around them. The shepherds were frightened. But the angel

said, 'Don't be afraid! I have good news for you, which will make everyone happy. This very day in King David's home town a Saviour was born for you. He is Christ the Lord. You will know who he is, because you will find him dressed in baby clothes and lying on a bed of hay.'

Suddenly many other angels came down from heaven and joined in praising God...

After the angels had left and gone back to heaven, the shepherds said to each other, 'Let's go to Bethlehem and see what the Lord has told us about.' They hurried off and found Mary and Joseph, and they saw the baby lying on a bed of hay.

When the shepherds saw Jesus, they told his parents what the angel had said about him. Everyone listened and was surprised. But Mary kept thinking about all this and wondering what it meant.

The wise men

When Jesus was born in the village of Bethlehem in Judea, Herod was king. During this time some wise men from the east came to Jerusalem and said, 'Where is the child born to be king of the Jews? We saw his star in the east and have come to worship him.'

When King Herod heard about this, he was worried, and so was everyone else in Jerusalem. Herod brought together the chief priests and the teachers of the Law of Moses and asked them, 'Where will the Messiah be born?'

They told him, 'He will be born in Bethlehem, just as the prophet wrote,

"Bethlehem in the land of Judea, you are very important among the towns of Judea. From your town will come a leader, who will be like a shepherd for my people Israel."'

Herod secretly called in the wise men and asked them when they had first seen the star. He told them, 'Go to Bethlehem and search carefully for the child. As soon as you find him, let me know. I want to go and worship him too.'

The wise men listened to what the king said and then left. And the star they had seen in the east went on ahead of them until it stopped over the place where the child was. They were thrilled and excited to see the star.

When the men went into the house and saw the child with Mary, his mother, they knelt down and worshipped him. They took out their gifts of gold, frankincense, and myrrh and gave them to him. Later they were warned in a dream not to return to Herod, and they went back home by another road.

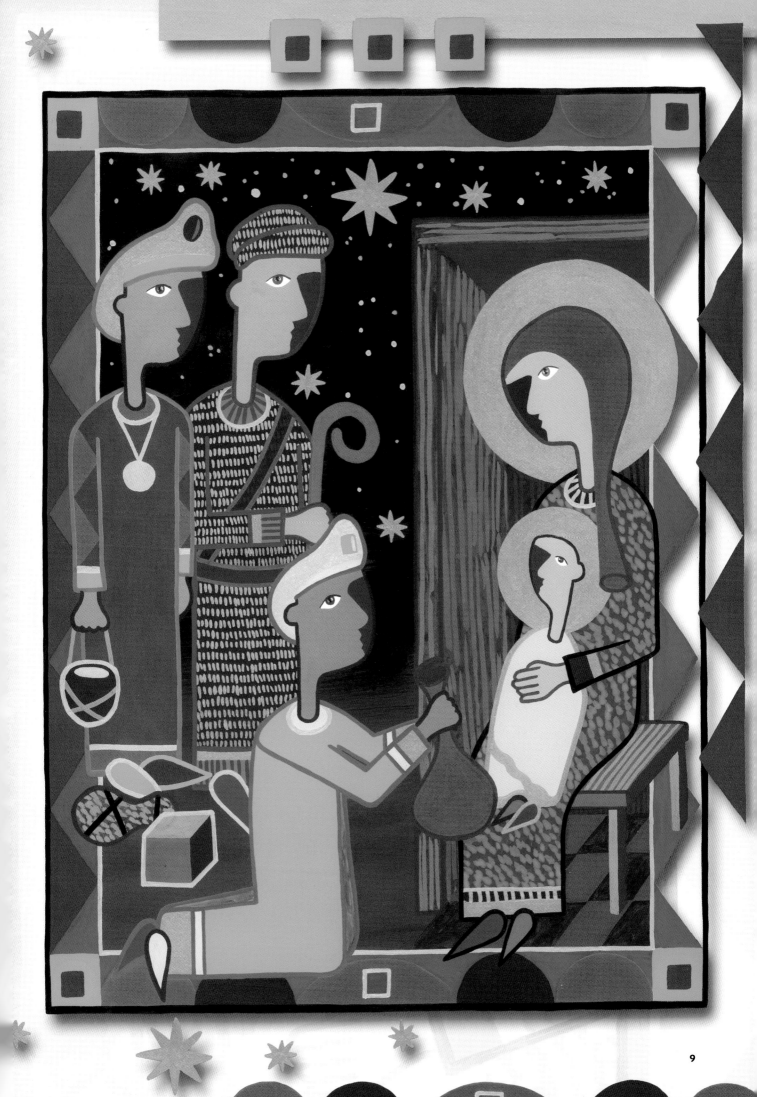

The killing of the children

MATTHEW 2:16–18

When Herod found out that the wise men from the east had tricked him, he was very angry. He gave orders for his men to kill all the boys who lived in or near Bethlehem and were two years old and younger. This was based on what he had learnt from the wise men.

So the Lord's promise came true, just as the prophet Jeremiah had said, 'In Ramah a voice was heard crying and weeping loudly. Rachel was mourning for her children, and she refused to be comforted, because they were dead.'

Simeon
praises the Lord

LUKE 2:22–35

T he time came for Mary and Joseph to do what the Law of Moses says a mother is supposed to do after her baby is born.

They took Jesus to the temple in Jerusalem and presented him to the Lord, just as the Law of the Lord says... The Law of the Lord also says that parents have to offer a sacrifice, giving at least a pair of doves or two young pigeons. So that is what Mary and Joseph did.

At this time a man named Simeon was living in Jerusalem. Simeon was a good man. He loved God and was waiting for God to save the people of Israel. God's Spirit came to him and told him that he would not die until he had seen Christ the Lord.

When Mary and Joseph brought Jesus to the temple to do what the Law of Moses says should be done for a new

baby, the Spirit told Simeon to go into the temple. Simeon took the baby Jesus in his arms and praised God,

'Lord, I am your servant, and now I can die in peace, because you have kept your promise to me. With my own eyes I have seen what you have done to save your people, and foreign nations will also see this. Your mighty power is a light for all nations, and it will bring honour to your people Israel.'

Jesus' parents were surprised at what Simeon had said. Then he blessed them and told Mary, 'This child of yours will cause many people in Israel to fall and others to stand. The child will be like a warning sign. Many people will reject him, and you, Mary, will suffer as though you had been stabbed by a dagger. But all this will show what people are really thinking.'

The boy Jesus in the temple

LUKE 2:41–52

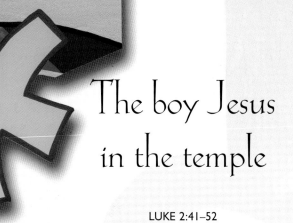

E very year Jesus' parents went to Jerusalem for Passover. And when Jesus was twelve years old, they all went there as usual for the celebration. After Passover his parents left, but they did not know that Jesus had stayed on in the city. They thought he was travelling with some other people, and they went a whole day before they started looking for him. When they could not find him with their relatives and friends, they went back to Jerusalem and started looking for him there.

Three days later they found Jesus sitting in the temple, listening to the teachers and asking them questions. Everyone who heard him was surprised at how much he knew and at the answers he gave.

When his parents found him, they were amazed. His mother said, 'Son, why have you done this to us? Your father and I have been very worried, and we have been searching for you!'

Jesus answered, 'Why did you have to look for me? Didn't you know that I would be in my Father's house?' But they did not understand what he meant.

Jesus went back to Nazareth with his parents and obeyed them. His mother kept on thinking about all that had happened.

Jesus became wise, and he grew strong. God was pleased with him and so were the people.

The baptism of Jesus

MATTHEW 3:13–17

 esus left Galilee and went to the River Jordan to be baptized by John. But John kept objecting and said, 'I ought to be baptized by you. Why have you come to me?'

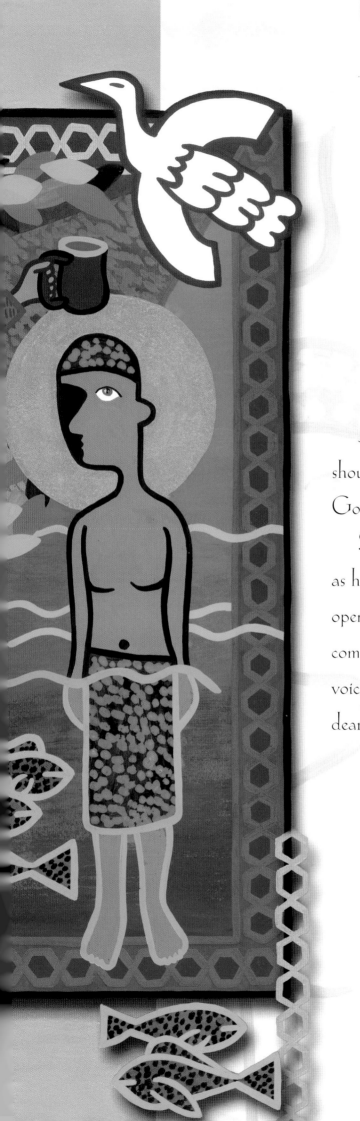

Jesus answered, 'For now this is how it should be, because we must do all that God wants us to do.' Then John agreed.

So Jesus was baptized. And as soon as he came out of the water, the sky opened, and he saw the Spirit of God coming down on him like a dove. Then a voice from heaven said, 'This is my own dear Son, and I am pleased with him.'

The temptations of Jesus

MATTHEW 4:1–11

T he Holy Spirit led Jesus into the desert, so that the devil could test him. After Jesus had gone without eating for forty days and nights, he was very

hungry. Then the devil came to him and said, 'If you are God's Son, tell these stones to turn into bread.'

Jesus answered, 'The Scriptures say: "No one can live only on food. People need every word that God has spoken."'

Next, the devil took Jesus to the holy city and made him stand on the highest part of the temple. The devil said, 'If you are God's Son, jump off. The Scriptures say:

"God will give his angels orders about you. They will catch you in their arms, and you won't hurt your feet on the stones."'

Jesus answered, 'The Scriptures also say, "Don't try to test the Lord your God!"'

Finally, the devil took Jesus up on a very high mountain and showed him all the kingdoms on earth and their power. The devil said to him, 'I will give all this to you, if you will bow down and worship me.'

Jesus answered, 'Go away Satan! The Scriptures say:

"Worship the Lord your God and serve only him."'

Then the devil left Jesus, and angels came to help him.

Jesus chooses his first disciples

LUKE 5:1–11

J esus was standing on the shore of Lake Gennesaret, teaching the people as they crowded around him to hear God's message. Near the shore he saw two boats left there by some fishermen who had gone to wash their nets. Jesus got into the boat that belonged to Simon and asked him to row it out a little way from the shore. Then Jesus sat down in the boat to teach the crowd.

When Jesus had finished speaking, he told Simon, 'Row the boat out into the deep water and let your nets down to catch some fish.'

'Master,' Simon answered, 'we have worked hard all night long and have not caught a thing. But if you tell me to, I will let the nets down.' They did it and caught so many fish that their nets began ripping apart. Then they signalled for their partners in the other boat to come and help them. The men came, and together they filled the two boats so full that they both began to sink.

When Simon Peter saw this happen, he knelt down in front of Jesus and said, 'Lord, don't come near me! I am a sinner.' Peter and everyone with him were completely surprised at all the fish they had caught. His partners James and John, the sons of Zebedee, were surprised too.

Jesus told Simon, 'Don't be afraid! From now on you will bring in people instead of fish.' The men pulled their boats up on the shore. Then they left everything and went with Jesus.

Jesus heals a man

MATTHEW 8:1–4

As Jesus came down the mountain, he was followed by large crowds. Suddenly a man with leprosy came and knelt in front of Jesus. He said, 'Lord, you have the power to make me well, if only you wanted to.'

Jesus put his hand on the man and said, 'I want to! Now you are well.' At once the man's leprosy disappeared. Jesus told him, 'Don't tell anyone about this, but go and show the priest that you are well. Then take a gift to the temple just as Moses commanded, and everyone will know that you have been healed.'

Jesus calms a storm

LUKE 8:22–25

ne day, Jesus and his disciples got into a boat, and he said, 'Let's cross the lake.' They started out, and while they were sailing across, he went to sleep.

Suddenly a storm struck the lake, and the boat started sinking. They were in danger. So they went to Jesus and woke him up, 'Master, Master! We are about to drown!'

Jesus got up and ordered the wind and waves to stop. They obeyed, and everything was calm. Then Jesus asked the disciples, 'Don't you have any faith?'

But they were frightened and amazed. They said to each other, 'Who is this? He can give orders to the wind and the waves, and they obey him!'

Jesus feeds five thousand

MATTHEW 14:13–21

A fter Jesus heard about John, he crossed Lake Galilee to go to some place where he could be alone. But the crowds found out and followed him on foot from the towns. When Jesus got out of the boat, he saw the large crowd. He felt sorry for them and healed everyone who was sick.

That evening the disciples came to Jesus and said, 'This place is like a desert, and it is already late. Let the crowds leave, so they can go to the villages and buy some food.'

Jesus replied, 'They don't
have to leave. Why don't you give
them something to eat?'

But they said, 'We have only five small
loaves of bread and two fish.' Jesus asked his
disciples to bring the food to him, and he told the
crowd to sit down on the grass. Jesus took the five loaves
and the two fish. He looked up towards heaven and blessed
the food. Then he broke the bread and handed it to his
disciples, and they gave it to the people.

After everyone had eaten all they wanted, Jesus' disciples
picked up twelve large baskets of leftovers.

There were about five thousand men who ate, not
counting the women and children.

The true glory
of Jesus

LUKE 9:28–36

About eight days later Jesus took
Peter, John, and James with him
and went up on a mountain to pray.
While he was praying, his face changed, and his

clothes became shining white. Suddenly Moses and Elijah were there speaking with him. They appeared in heavenly glory and talked about all that Jesus' death in Jerusalem would mean.

Peter and the other two disciples had been sound asleep. All at once they woke up and saw how glorious Jesus was. They also saw the two men who were with him.

Moses and Elijah were about to leave, when Peter said to Jesus, 'Master, it is good for us to be here! Let us make three shelters, one for you, one for Moses, and one for Elijah.' But Peter did not know what he was talking about.

While Peter was still speaking, a shadow from a cloud passed over them, and they were frightened as the cloud covered them. From the cloud a voice spoke, 'This is my chosen Son. Listen to what he says!'

After the voice had spoken, Peter, John, and James saw only Jesus. For some time they kept quiet and did not say anything about what they had seen.

Jesus enters Jerusalem

MATTHEW 21:1–11

When Jesus and his disciples came near Jerusalem, he went to Bethphage on the Mount of Olives and sent two of them on ahead. He told them, 'Go into the next village, where you will at once find a donkey and her colt. Untie the two donkeys and bring them to me. If anyone asks why you are doing that, just say, "The Lord needs them." Straight away he will let you have the donkeys.'

So God's promise came true, just as the prophet had said, 'Announce to the people of Jerusalem: "Your king is coming to you! He is humble and rides on a donkey. He comes on the colt of a donkey."'

The disciples left and did what Jesus had told them to do. They brought the donkey and its colt and laid some clothes on their backs. Then Jesus got on.

Many people spread clothes in the road, while others put down branches which they had cut from trees. Some people walked ahead of Jesus and others followed behind. They were all shouting,

'Hooray for the Son of David! God bless the one who comes in the name of the Lord. Hooray for God in heaven above!'

When Jesus came to Jerusalem, everyone in the city was excited and asked, 'Who can this be?'

The crowd answered, 'This is Jesus, the prophet from Nazareth in Galilee.'

Jesus washes the feet of his disciples

JOHN 13:4–12

During the meal Jesus got up, removed his outer garment, and wrapped a towel around his waist. He put some water into a large bowl. Then he began washing his disciples' feet and drying them with the towel he was wearing.

But when he came to Simon Peter, that disciple asked, 'Lord, are you going to wash my feet?'

Jesus answered, 'You don't really know what I am doing, but later you will understand.'

'You will never wash my feet!' Peter replied.

'If I don't wash you,' Jesus told him, 'you don't really belong to me.'

Peter said, 'Lord, don't wash just my feet. Wash my hands and my head.' Jesus answered, 'People who have bathed and are clean all over need to wash just their feet. And you, my disciples, are clean, except for one of you.' Jesus knew who would betray him. That is why he said, 'except for one of you.'

After Jesus had washed his disciples' feet and had put his outer garment back on, he sat down again.

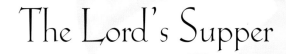

The Lord's Supper

MATTHEW 26:20–30

hen Jesus was eating with his twelve disciples that evening, he said, 'One of you will hand me over to my enemies.'

The disciples were very sad, and each one said to Jesus, 'Lord, you can't mean me!'

He answered, 'One of you men who has eaten with me from this dish will betray me. The Son of Man will die, as the Scriptures say. But it's going to be terrible for the one who betrays me! That man would be better off if he had never been born.'

Judas said, 'Teacher, surely you don't mean me!'

'That's what you say!' Jesus replied. But later, Judas did betray him.

During the meal Jesus took some bread in his hands. He blessed the bread and broke it. Then he gave it to his disciples and said, 'Take this and eat it. This is my body.'

Jesus picked up a cup of wine and gave thanks to God. He then gave it to his disciples and said, 'Take this and drink it. This is my blood, and with it God makes his agreement with you. It will be poured out, so that many people will have their sins forgiven. From now on I am not

going to drink any wine, until I drink new wine with you in my Father's kingdom.' Then they sang a hymn and went out to the Mount of Olives.

Jesus is arrested

esus was still speaking, when Judas the betrayer came up. He was one of the twelve disciples, and a large mob armed with swords and clubs was with him. They had been sent by the chief priests and the nation's leaders. Judas had told them beforehand, 'Arrest the man I greet with a kiss.'

Judas walked right up to Jesus and said, 'Hello, teacher.' Then Judas kissed him.

Jesus replied, 'My friend, why are you here?'

The men grabbed Jesus and arrested him. One of Jesus' followers pulled out a sword. He struck the servant of the high priest and cut off his ear.

But Jesus told him, 'Put your sword away. Anyone who lives by fighting will die by fighting. Don't you know that I could ask my Father, and straight away he would send me more than twelve armies of angels? But then, how could the words of the Scriptures come true, which say that this must happen?'

Jesus said to the mob, 'Why do you come with swords and clubs to arrest me like a criminal? Day after day I sat and taught in the temple, and you didn't arrest me. But all this happened, so that what the prophets wrote would come true.'

Pilate questions Jesus

MATTHEW 27:11–26

Jesus was brought before Pilate the governor, who asked him, 'Are you the king of the Jews?'

'Those are your words!' Jesus answered...

Pilate asked him, 'Don't you hear what crimes they say you have done?' But Jesus did not say anything, and the governor was greatly amazed.

During Passover the governor always freed a prisoner chosen by the people. At that time a well-known terrorist named Jesus Barabbas was in jail. So when the crowd came together, Pilate asked them, 'Which prisoner do you want me to set free? Do you want Jesus Barabbas or Jesus who is called the Messiah?' Pilate knew that the leaders had brought Jesus to him because they were jealous.

While Pilate was judging the case, his wife sent him a message. It said, 'Don't have anything to do with that innocent man. I have had nightmares because of him.'

But the chief priests and the leaders convinced the crowds to ask for Barabbas to be set free and for Jesus to be killed. Pilate asked the crowd again, 'Which of these two men do you want me to set free?'

'Barabbas!' they replied.

Pilate asked them, 'What am I to do with Jesus, who is called the Messiah?'

They all yelled, 'Nail him to a cross!'

Pilate answered, 'But what crime has he done?'

'Nail him to a cross!' they yelled even louder.

Pilate saw that there was nothing he could do and that the people were starting to riot. So he took some water and washed his hands in front of them and said, 'I won't

have anything to do with killing this man. You are the
ones doing it!' ...

Pilate set Barabbas free. Then he ordered his soldiers
to beat Jesus with a whip and nail
him to a cross.

Jesus is nailed to a cross

MATTHEW 27:31–54

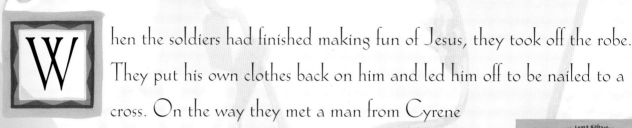

W hen the soldiers had finished making fun of Jesus, they took off the robe. They put his own clothes back on him and led him off to be nailed to a cross. On the way they met a man from Cyrene named Simon, and they forced him to carry Jesus' cross.

They came to a place named Golgotha, which means 'Place of a Skull'. There they gave Jesus some wine mixed with a drug to ease the pain. But… he refused to drink it.

The soldiers nailed Jesus to a cross and gambled to see who would get his clothes.

Then they sat down to guard him. Above his head they put a sign that told why he was nailed there. It read, 'This is Jesus, the King of the Jews.' The soldiers also nailed two criminals on crosses…

People who passed by said terrible things about Jesus. They shook their heads and shouted, 'So you're the one who claimed you could tear down the temple and build it again in three days! If you are God's Son, save yourself and come down from the cross!'

The chief priests, the leaders, and the teachers of the Law of Moses also made fun of Jesus…

At midday the sky turned dark and stayed that way until three o'clock. Then about that time Jesus shouted, 'Eli, Eli, lema sabachthani?' which means, 'My God, my

eli, eli, lama sabachthani?

God, why have you deserted me?'

Some of the people standing there heard Jesus... One of them at once ran and grabbed a sponge. He soaked it in wine, then put it on a stick and held it up to Jesus... Once again Jesus shouted, and then he died.

At once the curtain in the temple was torn in two from top to bottom. The earth shook, and rocks split apart... The officer and the soldiers guarding Jesus felt the earthquake and saw everything else that happened. They were frightened and said, 'This man really was God's Son!'

Jesus is alive

MARK 16:1–8

After the Sabbath, Mary Magdalene, Salome, and Mary the mother of James bought some spices to put on Jesus' body. Very early on Sunday morning, just as the sun was coming up, they went to the tomb. On their way, they were asking one another, 'Who will roll the stone away from the entrance for us?' But when they looked, they saw that the stone had already been rolled away. And it was a huge stone!

The women went into the tomb, and on the right side they saw a young man in a white robe sitting there.

They were alarmed.

The man said, 'Don't be alarmed! You are looking for Jesus from Nazareth, who was nailed to a cross. God has raised him to life, and he isn't here. You can see the place where they put his body. Now go and tell his disciples, and especially Peter, that he will go ahead of you to Galilee. You will see him there, just as he told you.'

When the women ran from the tomb, they were confused and shaking all over. They were too afraid to tell anyone what had happened.

Jesus and Thomas

lthough Thomas the Twin was one of the twelve disciples, he wasn't with the others when Jesus appeared to them. So they told him, 'We have seen the Lord!'

But Thomas said, 'First, I must see the nail scars in his hands and touch them with my finger. I must put my hand where the spear went into his side. I won't believe unless I do this!'

A week later the disciples were together again. This time, Thomas was with them. Jesus came in while the doors were still locked and stood in the middle of the group. He greeted his disciples and said to Thomas, 'Put your finger here and look at my hands! Put your hand into my side. Stop doubting and have faith!'

Thomas replied, 'You are my Lord and my God!'

Jesus said, 'Thomas, do you have faith because you have seen me? The people who have faith in me without seeing me are the ones who are really blessed!'

The coming of the Holy Spirit

ACTS 2:1–12

On the day of Pentecost all the Lord's followers were together in one place. Suddenly there was a noise from heaven like the sound of a mighty wind! It filled the house where they were meeting. Then they saw what looked like fiery tongues moving in all directions, and a tongue came and settled on each person there. The Holy Spirit took control of everyone, and they began speaking whatever languages the Spirit let them speak.

Many religious Jews from every country in the world were living in Jerusalem. And when they heard this noise, a crowd gathered. But they were surprised, because they were hearing everything in their own languages. They were excited and amazed, and said:

Don't all these who are speaking come from Galilee? Then why do we hear them speaking our very own languages? Some of us are from Parthia, Media, and Elam. Others are from Mesopotamia, Judea, Cappadocia, Pontus, Asia, Phrygia, Pamphylia, Egypt, parts of Libya near Cyrene, Rome, Crete, and Arabia. Some of us were born Jews, and others of us have chosen to be Jews. Yet we all hear them using our own languages to tell the wonderful things God has done.

Everyone was excited and confused. Some of them even kept asking each other, 'What does all this mean?'

Illustrations copyright © Paul Forsey 2004

Published by
The Bible Reading Fellowship
First Floor, Elsfield Hall
15-17 Elsfield Way, Oxford OX2 8FG

ISBN 1 84101 330 7
First published 2004
10 9 8 7 6 5 4 3 2 1 0

Acknowledgments
Unless otherwise stated, scripture quotations are taken from the Contemporary
English Version of the Bible published by HarperCollins Publishers,
copyright © 1991, 1992, 1995 American Bible Society.

A catalogue record for this book is available from the British Library

Printed and bound in China